between the couch cushions

written by
claudia m divincenzo

cover art by
brenda divincenzo

Copyright © 2021 by Claudia DiVincenzo

All rights reserved. No part of this book may be reproduced or used in any manner without written permission of the copyright owner except for the use of quotations in a book review.

FIRST EDITION

Cover art by Brenda DiVincenzo
Edited by Emme Woodward

ISBN 9781070966274 (paperback)

This is a work of fiction. Names, characters, places, and incidents either are the product of the author's imagination or are used fictitiously. Any resemblance to actual persons, living or dead, events, or locales is entirely coincidental.

dedication

to all my loved ones. you made this book possible. although I am the one who wrote these words, the words would not have been written without you. my creation began with you. and now it lives in your hands.

thank you for giving me the courage to write the book that my heart has been telling me to write all my life. your support brings the stars within reach.

adrift in sunset blush

I am engulfed by the words I long to say,
endlessly clinging to my raft of silence
in the vast ocean of my unspoken desires,
spitting salt water into lies.
I have been left to drown by many others,
sailors who feared these perilous waters
and the truths that swim below my feet,
those great barracudas.
I have drifted for many years in this sea,
navigating the ways in which I am quiet
and searching for a shore where I might rest
to tell you of my ocean.

hippodrome

I am advised to be careful
in the ways I move about the world.

We cannot know what the men
may do, I am told.

They are never advised
the same of me.

They believe the things I hold
must not be worth much in my hand.

If I can wield it,
it must be a meager sword.

They have much to say about
the woman with the weapon.

Had I forged this blade,
toiled long with blackened hands,

it would be taken from me
and gifted to a more capable grip,

or tossed far out to the sea nymphs,
in fear that my touch may besmirch.

But I have grown weary of weakness,
of feigning these niceties;

c.m.d

I am grasping the hilt of this blade,
and raising my fist to the air.

The arena is silent
no longer.

lost petals

I have either dropped them carelessly
somewhere along the road,

lost them in the distracting caress
of a late evening's wind,

gifted them to a weary traveler
in need of nature's quiet comfort,

or you have plucked them off
in a game of *I love her,
I love her not.*

Either way—
spring has come and I stand bare;

it doesn't quite matter anymore
how exactly it came to pass.

introvert

I don't have much to say
in the midst of it all;
when people are pouring words
down each other's throats
to chase the booze they are guzzling,
I am probably watching and giggling
and thinking about something else
that has nothing to do with anything
regarding the current moment.

I am someone else entirely
in the face of an empty page;
when the void of silence presented
is quite literally palpable
there remains the best listener of all.
I am probably churning and smiling
and writing about all the things
I was thinking before, when
there were dozens of people around
but no ears to be found.

it's all in vain

We spend nights pressed together
like grapes into wine
on a vine still aching to grow
into something more.

I have already been pressed too thin
and bled dry many a time,
so it's truly all in vain
to think I could survive off the vine.

addendum

I pick up my pen to mention you
and it either comes out sounding like
you meant the world
or nothing at all,
and neither I can say
are very true.

depression

I am joined at the hips by bones that creak,
reminded that age matters on rainy days I spend
scraping the cocoa from the bottom of my mug
and burning poor incense that embeds the walls
with a campfire scent.

We stick our noses in time only to ask
how much of it is left,
capered in youth by the idea of buying more,
minds in thrall on shelves of riddled wood
waiting for someone important
to see us as such, too.

I am indebted to a new resolution every day,
capping my ability at accomplishing small feats;
today it is to write a proud verse of which I may lay
my fatigue on, a small woolen blanket for anxieties unmet;
tomorrow it may be to just get out of bed.

c.m.d

how to comfort a friend

The door is not for you to open,
it is for them to let you in.

Your knock may be ignored
if you are impatient with the rain.

The coat-rack is not for your jacket,
but for the judgment you may pass.

You may be asked to leave
if you forget to hang it up.

The silence is not for you to fill,
it is for them to share with you.

You may not be asked to stay
if you claim it as your own.

c.m.d

a chance encounter

Unlike the ones before you,
you were not rough on the edges.

You didn't cut me
every time you touched me
and your words didn't burn,
they were simply warm
on the nape of my neck.

We slipped right past one another,
two smooth stones in a raging river.

c.m.d

a new day

I think that people are going to crawl
out of drains and gutters for you
because I brought the rain with me
and they're asking to see the sun.

confession

Writing poetry
used to make me
feel brave.

It felt
like a war cry
on a blank page.

It felt
like I had finally
crawled from a cave.

But now—

Writing poetry
feels like
another fence.

It is not
a battle call,
but a wary defense.

Each line I compose
constructs a levee
of metaphoric pretense.

ice sculpture

You don't need anyone else
to complete you, she told me.

I know that, I replied.
But what about needing someone
for something else?

Like what? she asked.

Like maybe just someone
to take an ice pick to my bones,
to shatter me a little,
possibly a lot,
so I can figure out the pieces I need
and which ones I'm supposed to
leave behind.

mortar and pestle

It is not unbearable:
the way you grind my bones
under an angry gaze.
Bruises sprout like cute little pop-ups
in my favorite childhood book,
but flipping the pages
can't make them disappear
anymore.
It isn't all for naught:
I have sometimes loved
being dust.

c.m.d

today

It starts, in part, when the day begins—
I look at my calendar and put on an appropriate mood.
The morning sticks like honey drizzled in steaming tea,
Nearly forgotten to be stirred in but melting all the same.
We speak in silence before 8 am—
My brain wakes with the sun, later in the winter.

I find your shoes next to mine on the welcome mat—
When did you become so familiar here?
I grant the teabag an apology when I drop it in the trash,
Half-seeped, *I am running late again.*
I spend free thoughts on you during midday—
They pay me good money to keep the rest in my cubicle.

dry fruit

I don't think that much else
could've come from us
if we had put all our parts
into a juicer.
no different from before,
we would still be the same:
we were both already
drained.

morning of the dead

We sift the morning air
like the sky is holding secrets,
searching for words
where others search for God.
Yet all we've found
is last night's residue
still stuck to our lips
like resin from the music
we made together
under the sheets.
To leave this early
would be rude to the rooster,
he has waited all night
for his moment to shine.
Yet my skin is tight
on my bones
like I am a present
wrapped in tearing tissue paper.
I think I would speak easier
with a knife in my mouth,
but I know from the way
you are looking at the door,
either way I will still bleed today.

c.m.d

reminder

You are not his mother tasked
to dress him in kindness

He is not a window mannequin
for you to clothe into comfort

Anger is not a sweater
you can ask him to take off

between the couch cushions

I am afraid I have lost something
in the gap between our hearts.
It slipped down, unnoticed,
between the seats and has made a home
with other forgotten things.

aging

I toss in my sleep and then wake
to my hip popping and complaining,
asking where you are,
why you aren't here to kiss it
in its lonely agony.
My bones are sore in your absence,
they creak and crack more often
and while I am only twenty,
it feels I am growing so old,
so ancient and outdated
without you.

silent window

It no longer holds your silhouette in its pane,
instead it breathes in the bugs and lets the rain
cling to it—wanting to become a home again.

pottery

I am hard to find in my bones,
these warped cavities,
too worn from being spun
in the same spot
again and again.
What shape was I
before this molding storm?

propagation

I hope you placed
the parts of me you took
in water.

I hope they are happy
on your kitchen windowsill,
in the old mason jar
you used to trap beetles in
when you were young.

I hope you at least
take care of the things
you stole.

I hope you pay attention
when a new sprout emerges,
when the leaf unfurls
and shows a benign face
not unlike my own.

I hope you find growth
in the parts of me that survived
your departure.

barefoot

When you step across the bedlam,
do you see how fleeting
reprieve can become?

In the silence after every storm,
you feel the warm touch of serenity
on your tired cheek,

but it does not soothe you
in the way you thought it would.

The visions of reconciliation
you harbored so vehemently
have become an accelerant

in the moments of quiet,
when you are holding your cheek
with delusional comfort

wondering from which direction
the next blizzard will strike you from.

We who love you, ask you:

Do not settle for the momentary warmth
of an apologetic smile
when it is always preluded

by the cold bite of unsettled anger.
You have asked for the road to peace;
and yet, you have chosen to walk barefoot

c.m.d

in the uncharted biting brush
instead of on the path
carved by the ones who cherish you.

c.m.d

the courier

My arms are heavy
from all the pieces of you
that need to be held.

c.m.d

erosion

You loved me as the river
loves the canyon:

a force of nature
that hugged the walls
of my soul

just long enough
to carve a path to the ocean.

unrequited

I know I will always be behind glass,
a mannequin to be admired in the mornings
you forget that you cannot touch me.

I hold my limbs in ways I've seen dolls do,
an array of petite decorations in a window
I am happy to stay silent behind.

c.m.d

the threshold

I have not emptied my heart
while around you before—
this is nearly worse
than spilling my purse.

I am rushing to grab things
before you spot them
until I notice your hands
beside mine on the rug.

And it comes to me later
that I knew you would carry
any of the things inside me
without complaint.

I had not emptied my heart
while around you before—
but now I think I find
that I didn't quite mind.

c.m.d

the minimalist

Being the way that I am:
I won't forget you if you don't forget me,
won't move on from you if you don't from me;
the flower of my love will continue to blossom
with whatever little rain you deem it deserves.
My body can survive on so little, I think:
I may as well live the life of a diagnosed minimalist.
If you spare me the remnants,
those I will take without complaint or question.
I cannot appreciate this about myself,
but I must warn you; I must say,

Being the way that I am:
I won't hesitate to forget you if you forget me,
will move on surely if you do so from me;
if no rain from you is sent my way,
I have no issue in uprooting my flower
to find somewhere that has what it needs.
My body can survive on so little, I think:
I may live as a minimalist but I cannot live with nothing.
So once you are gone,
know that I have already forgotten you.

atrophy

She looks in the mirror
and sees the wilt:

eyes casting shadows
that could shade the pines
outside her window.

c.m.d

suture

There is a thread loose
in my mustard sweater,
pulled from its place
by my cat's clawing reach.

I leave it there
for a week or two
until it gets caught
on the car door
and then it's too late
to go find the scissors.

There is a thought loose
in my raucous head,
pulled from its place
by a faded memory.

I leave it there
for a week or two
until it gets caught
on the rest of my brain
and unravels the stitching
I had so gingerly sewn.

washed and dried

Nothing sticks, not even us.
Everything comes out
in the wash: your lips,
my laughs. enveloped in
your favorite shirt, the one
you gave to me, our moments
were an object to be traded,
to be shrunk in the dryer and
faded after each use.
Do you think she'll recognize
the signs like I did?
It doesn't matter how many
cranberry kisses you share,
everything comes out
in the wash: your lips,
her laughs. The dryer
will shrink the pleasure
between her thighs
when she realizes you spilled
lies on the shirt you
gave her (after me).

goodbye

On my window
the clouds run their tears
down my translucent reflection,
collecting in watery freckles
on the sky's dark face outside.
I see you
standing down below
waiting for me to let you in,
but I draw the blinds instead
and hope the bleeding rain
on the window pane
doesn't make it seem
as if I am in the same sorrow
as the clouds are.

analgesia

If you twist the blade in
just a bit further,
maybe I would finally
notice the wound.

If you leave it in the skin
just a bit longer,
maybe I would finally
find this crimson origin.

c.m.d

bruised by the horizon

The sun is a tangerine hanging lonely in the sky
waiting to be peeled and enjoyed by the sunset,

in much the same way I have been waiting, too.
I think about maybe staying for the rest of the day

to watch it float in its waterless ocean,
when I am reminded of something on my list

I forgot to do.
You tell me not to worry,

because that's the thing about the sun:
it will be there tomorrow to watch,

and the day after, if I so desire.
And yes, it most likely will be, I agree.

Until maybe one day
it's not.

stardust

If I feel you
trying to pry me open,
I'm afraid I'll explode
into useless powder,
unable to manifest
into the star I long to be.

chroma

I am play-doh in your hands,
but you like to mash
the colors together,

and now there are things inside me
I will never be able
to pick out.

small talk

I am told I have
lost it again:
that contemplative touch
I adhere to my tone
to seem just slightly enamored
by the nonsense you spill;
in any other case I would
turn off the tap to save a mess
but your kind of babble
is amusing to dabble in,
occasionally.

styx

Some nights
I dream of my mother
carrying me to the river
at the world's edge
and dipping my golden head
into its eternal current,
a babe as blessed as Achilles.

Other nights
I feel each broken piece
carrying me back to you
on a slim promise
bruising my mortal heart
under your eternal current,
a woman as weak as the warrior's heel.

body talk

Words scratching against
my throat like sandpaper:
this is hard.

Nails cutting the palms
of my hands like knives:
but I want to know you.

No response.

I want to love you,
give me a chance.

The mirror said nothing,
but the girl in it
whispered:
okay.

china doll

I point to the cracks near my chest.
they splinter out like tree branches,
with dangerous arms that threaten
to break me every time I move.

These were my first, I say
and they hurt the most.

Then to the chip on my elbow.
It dips into my arm like a soup bowl,
with a smaller one partnered beside it
to remind me that no pain is ever singular.

These were from falling, I say
but I got back up.

summer of '09

Fruit flies trapped in the jelly jar
that my father set out last Tuesday
collect in an amber grave

I am rooting through my mother's closet

There must've been a time she wore
these dangling globe earrings
and spun them on their tiny hooks
little mobile planets waiting
to be pinched into place

Downstairs I hear the porch door slam
and the dog's chain is yanking her
from digging in the garden again

The hooks pinch my squeezed palms

Trickling blood along my life lines
these little planets browse my skin
and spin against my fingertips
continents so small and thin
I clutch them into dust

midnight snack

Every time I find something we share
I want to tuck it away behind my ear
for my heart to snack on later
because nothing makes me hungrier for you
than the ways in which we are the same.

c.m.d

beginning

Let me crawl into the creases
underneath your eyes,
enveloped in your smile
for the days to come—
life seems more bearable
this way.

silent film

My mirror knows nothing
of the things I keep inside.
It knows only what catches
in its frame:
the edge of my bed,
the philodendron that spreads
near the north window,
the bookcase that houses
the words I like to
escape to.
My mirror knows nothing
of beauty beyond my bedroom.
It sees only what passes through
its gold frame:
my exhaustion at day's end,
the worry that has made a home
on my forehead,
the soft smile I give when
I am sad
and you call me.

c.m.d

my cat, salem

It is important business,
his morning conversation
with the sun.

He wonders where it goes
deep in the day,
why it wanes in such a way
before he is done with it.

They have much to discuss,
regarding the ways of the world
beyond the welcome mat.

He slips behind the yellow curtains
to catch the daybreak's yawn,
a warden of the withering lawn
and the flitting cowbirds it holds.

It is tiring business,
his morning conversation
with the sun.

He sneaks away to his pillow
when the colloquy runs dry,
a soft jingle and a sigh
before he tucks his head.

on nights I read my old journals

This is my favorite place to loot:
yellowed pages guarded by
an armored history and sometimes
there is a feeble drawing of swords,
but the present always manages
to strike down whatever the past
may have had to offer, in the end.

Stealing from this place
could not be considered thievery:
these thoughts are no longer wanted
or needed.

Instead, I muse over the items:
the broken spirit rudely stitched
back together by various tradesmen,
the starving heart eventually appeased
from within its own cavities,
and the aching hand flawlessly cured
through flaunts of vigorous scrawling.

This is where the discovery lies:
recognizing that the terrain of today
was built by the winds, floods, and storms
of yesterday.

c.m.d

old skin

I could have lived anywhere
or they like to tell me so anyway,

I don't quite see how I could have
lived with you much longer.

You pinched me all the time
as if you didn't like me much either,

I don't quite blame you
I was a nuisance boxed up like that.

paper love

We can live
like two paper planes
searching for each other
in the infinite space.
Joined by the wind patterns
carved by the earth
and parted the same way,
a never-ending search.

requiem

Tonight seems a good night
to hollow me out
with your fingertips,
gentle like ginger spice
sprinkled over days
we spent under a sky
tainted orange—hue of
a goodnight kiss that
turned into farewell.

letter to a past self

You didn't think
I would make it this far
and you were halfway right;
I had to crawl on some occasions,
with knees rubbed raw and scabbed palms.

And I admit
even after new skin grew
erasing all traces of the journey,
there are days I am unsure I travel lighter,
when I reach to ease a phantom weight.

So today I turn my head
back down the road I have come
to thank you for all that you shouldered;
you have shaped a girl scared of her shadow
into a woman able to bear the weight of her future.

one size too big

I can't remember a time
when the world seemed big enough
to fill the shoes of my dreams.
I am told there is room to grow,
but I am not told when
the growing season will begin.
My feet are swimming in pools
I cried when I was young,
stagnant in their dormant journey.
Life is budding on these soaked soles,
but how long can it last
before drowning alongside my toes.

grow light

I find a hand to grasp
in the trees,
tall limbs reaching
towards the sky's face
in a lifelong caress.
Is it calming,
I wonder,
to have always known
which path
will give you life?

shiver

Tonight is the kind of kiss
that leaves a chill behind
on a tranquil mind.

c.m.d

guidebook to growing up

Because you're only a teenager, you don't know yourself.
And don't think that
You can do what they say you cannot.

Do what others tell you without question.
And do not ever permit yourself to
Believe you're smart enough to make your own decisions.

Because he was nice to you, you owe him.
And do not consider that
You are allowed to leave without giving him anything.

Easy girls are more attractive.
And do not dare to think that
Saying "no" is acceptable.

You are only worth what you can offer him.
And don't believe that
You'll still be valuable when he doesn't want you anymore.

To be happy, all you have to do is try not to be sad.
And don't believe people who say that
Any mental illness is as important as a physical ailment.

Because you're only a teenager, you don't know yourself.
And do not ever start to believe that
You are important to this world.

(now read from bottom to top)

c.m.d

letting go

Here's what I think—
you are wondering
when you will know
if someone fits right,

because sometimes
the piece kind of belongs,
if you try to make it,
maybe bend it a little

and yeah sure it's fine,
it looks a bit off but maybe
it was a just a slight
manufacturing mistake,

the colors align,
after all.

Here's what I think—
you've probably forgotten
it's a bit misshaped
after all this time,

because it doesn't bode well
to dally in one spot
when the rest of the picture
is gaping in a blank stare

and yeah sure sometimes
it pops out of place
and you're tired so
you ask it to please stay,

c.m.d

it isn't needed anywhere else
at the moment.

Here's what I think—
you will probably believe
that piece is the right choice
until you find one that fits better,

because you couldn't possibly know
what the finished product needed
at the soft beginning
of this life.

and yeah sure
it will feel strange
to pull it out of the scene's grasp
and see the void it leaves,

but that emptiness makes room
for something snug.

c.m.d

island

Have I really healed
if I still swim out here sometimes
to be alone and reopen
the wounds that stranded me here
in the first place?

nebula

Your shoulder, bare,
holds a freckled constellation
untouched by the darkness
that other stars are subject to.

odyssey

I do not know
if it was Poseidon's mercy
that brought me to you
on the cobalt waves,
or perhaps instead his anger
at my mortal presence
so stagnant on the surf
of his children.

And I cannot forget
the aid of Aeolus' grace
that pushed me to you
as keeper of the winds,
or perhaps it was Helios
who finally grew weary
of my shameless basking
under his chariot's belly.

But I am not inclined
to question the methods
of the eternally divine,
for perhaps it was not they
but you who gripped the seas
and wielded the winds
and shouldered the sun
to find me.

poem in duo

The pain
will end

and the
sky will
not split

and the
earth will
not crumble.

The rain
will not
last forever.

The plants
will not
hold your
ache in
their roots,

the bees
will not
come to
pollinate the
agony you
grow here.

The only
home for
the pain
you hold
is you.

c.m.d

And so,
when you
have run
dry from
its seep,

when your
hands are
cracked from
its heat,

call up
the strength
you need,

the power
that lives
deep underneath,

and banish
it from
your hallowed
bleeding grounds,
unburden your
soul as
it takes
its leave.

Because you,
I promise,
have somewhere
much better
to be.

about the author

Claudia DiVincenzo was born in December of 1997. She has loved writing her whole life, and highly suspects she loved it in all of her past lives as well. Claudia has a Bachelor of Science in Psychology from the University of Tennessee at Chattanooga, where she spent a great deal of time learning all the ways in which people are different. And yet, she hopes that every one of her readers can find a piece of themselves somewhere within the pages of *between the couch cushions*. When she isn't writing or reading, she enjoys playing video games, tending to her many houseplants, and loving on her cat, Salem.

Made in the USA
Columbia, SC
30 April 2021